abc's
of
Short-Wave Listening

by Len Buckwalter

HOWARD W. SAMS & CO., INC.
THE BOBBS-MERRILL CO., INC.
INDIANAPOLIS · KANSAS CITY · NEW YORK

THIRD EDITION

SECOND PRINTING—1971

International Standard Book Number: 0-672-20797-4
Library of Congress Catalog Card Number: 72-128119

Contents

Preface

Short-wave radio has given rise to a breed of armchair adventurers who roam the world with a twist of a dial on a radio receiver. Few events are barred from the ears of the avid listener—from the anxious distress call of a sinking ship to the weird beeping from an orbiting satellite.

Short wave is widely used as a means of both emergency and routine two-way communications; marine, aviation, and law-enforcement radios are active in various parts of the short-wave bands. With a little skill the listener can tune in behind the scenes at a busy airport, a rescue operation at sea, a civil defense hurricane operation, or anywhere there is a need for outside help.

But there is much more than just excitement on the short-wave bands; the busy wavelengths abound in programs of entertainment and educational value. Many are transmitted in English from such distant points as Tokyo, London, Moscow, Paris, Berlin, and Manila. If a foreign language is what you want, there are short-wave transmitters in practically every country on earth. All these and many more fascinating programs are beamed by commercial stations directly to you, the short-wave listener.

The wonderful thing about short-wave broadcasts is that there is almost no limit to the distance they can travel. When atmospheric conditions are most favorable (and they change from hour to hour), a relatively low-powered transmitter can be picked up by a sensitive receiver just about anywhere. Part of the challenge of short-wave listening is to see how many different places are represented by the stations that can be received.

This new edition has been prepared because of the widespread interest in short wave. All the information in the tables and charts has been brought up to date so it will continue to be useful for reference. New developments in equipment are also included.

The key to this wonderful world of short-wave listening is yours for the asking—just a small investment in some modest equipment and the desire to discover the world from the comfort of your own home.

LEN BUCKWALTER

CHAPTER 1

Short-Wave Listening

Three faint pulses of sound announced the birth of short-wave radio in 1901. Encamped on Signal Hill in the southeastern corner of Canada, Guglielmo Marconi strained to hear the first trans-Atlantic radio signals from England. During this historic moment, Marconi demonstrated to the world that radio was not merely a laboratory curiosity capable of limited range, but rather a revolutionary new medium for global communications.

Although Marconi's feat excited people everywhere, it literally rocked the scientific world. Distinguished physicists were virtually unanimous in their reaction: "Mathematically impossible," they said. It was generally believed that radio, like light, travelled in perfectly straight lines. Thus, it could not curve over the earth's surface to form a link between two distant points. Scientific reasoning suggested that a signal from England would shoot off into space and never reach Canada. Further doubt was created by the fact that no one ventured a plausible explanation for the strange behavior of radio waves in Marconi's experiment.

Obviously, the scientists were wrong since Marconi continued to conquer great distances with his primitive equipment. The first inkling of an explanation stirred in 1902. While aboard the ocean liner *Philadelphia,* Marconi observed that messages could be received successfully from distances of 700 miles during the day and 2,000 miles at night. In some way radio waves were being affected by the earth's atmosphere. Stimulated by this steady build-up of evidence, scientists began to sprout theories. Both A. E. Kennelly and O. Heaviside, while working independently of each other, soon came up with the idea of an electrical region high in the earth's atmosphere that could act like a mirror to radio waves. Instead of heading into space, radio-wave energy would be reflected back to the earth where it could be received by a distant station. As a tribute to the correctness of the idea, the region was designated the Kennelly-Heaviside layer. Today it is more commonly called the *ionosphere.* The special behavior of this electrified region is largely responsible for short-wave radio.

By 1925 careful measurements of the ionosphere had been taken. Through a process of beaming brief radio pulses to the upper layers of the atmosphere, returning echoes yielded extensive information about the nature of the ionosphere. Scientists soon conceived the overall picture of a huge umbrella-like layer over much of the earth. This layer invisibly ebbed and flowed with the passing days and seasons. They noted that certain radio frequencies passed through unobstructed, while others were reflected at various angles. Once the secrets of the ionosphere were laid bare, the next 50 years witnessed tremendous development in the field of long-distance communications. Even today rockets and satellites probe the region to add to the existing store of information.

Thus the field of short-wave radio was born, and with it was ushered in the fascinating hobby of short-wave listening (Fig. 1-1). As an increasing number of stations took to the air in the 1920's, people thrilled to sounds which they knew had originated many miles way. For some it provided their first contact with people, places, and events far beyond the area in which they lived. Others took to short-wave listening who enjoyed the technical challenge of building equipment capable of receiving distant signals.

Fig. 1-1. The short-wave fan finds colorful listening day or night.

Short-wave listening (SWL) is enjoyed today with all the excitement discovered by the "old timers" several generations ago. It is a field that constantly grows, offering the SWL'er an increasing number of ways in which he can enjoy his hobby within the comforts of his own home. Early equipment with its tricky *cat's whisker* adjustments and costly battery has been replaced by the infinitely more sensitive superhet receiver. In addition, the hobbyist no longer has to operate during late evening hours to pick up isolated stations. Throughout the day and night the wide coverage of the SW receiver brings in distant signals at many points on the dial.

In contrast to bygone days, there are now over 3,000 stations broadcasting to the world's short-wave listeners. Operating at high power, they fill the wavelengths with programs of every conceivable type. Consider the British Broadcasting Corporation (BBC), whose "External Programme Operations" began regular service to the world in 1932 (Fig. 1-2). Operating 37 powerful transmitters in England, the BBC output reaches the staggering figure of over 500 hours per week! Through a system of eight networks, programs are

Courtesy British Broadcasting Corporation

Fig. 1-2. "Dateline London" is one of hundreds of programs broadcast by BBC, one of the world's leading short-wave networks. Shown are host Lee Hamilton and Julie Andrews.

Courtesy Radiodiffusion-Télévision Francaise

Fig. 1-3. A powerful short-wave station in France presents the language course: "French by Radio."

broadcast in forty-one different languages. Thousands of people the world over tune to the BBC especially to hear the newscasts, which are noted for their accuracy and impartiality. They are delivered at the rate of 1,000 per week on a global basis. The BBC schedule also includes many programs of cultural and educational value.

The strong voice of the French Broadcasting System also beams programs to the short-wave listener (Fig. 1-3). A huge half-million–watt facility at Allouis, France, transmits regularly in French and English to the North American continent. Also, Radio Moscow delivers a considerable number of newscasts and reports of industrial and scientific progress —all intended to propagandize the American listener with the Soviet point of view.

Whatever your interest, you'll probably find it covered on the short-wave bands: a talk on West Indian wrestling, a lesson in Japanese with Dr. Toru Matsumoto (Fig. 1-4), or perhaps jazz played Dutch style. There's opera, folk music, symphonic works, popular tunes, and talks on stamp collecting and literature. Radio Nigeria offers a community sing. Radio Manila sounds the "Call of the Orient," and Radio Japan conducts a guided tour through points of interest in the Japanese islands. The bands are literally filled with programs of education and information (Fig. 1-5), and there is no language barrier. A large portion of the broadcasts from world capitals are in English, particularly if they are beamed toward the United States. Of course, if you are learning a foreign language, a short-wave receiver affords a marvelous pronunciation guide. Just listen to the country of your choice.

Short-wave listening is not restricted to the outpouring of international broadcast stations. Dotted throughout the bands is a myriad of communications services that often af-

Courtesy Nippon Hoso Kyokai

Fig. 1-4. "Let's Speak Japanese" is beamed to America twice a week from Tokyo for the English-speaking audience.

ford exciting listening (Fig. 1-6). Hundreds of SWL'ers heard the dramatic distress call and rescue operations the night the Andrea Doria sank after a collision at sea. The marine frequencies also bring the chatter of tugboat captains or reports of fishing conditions from commercial and pleasure boats. Aviation enthusiasts can eavesdrop on airport control

Courtesy Radio Corporation of America International

Fig. 1-5. Performers in Karachi before the microphones of Radio Pakistan.

towers or hear the voices of pilots as they fly over the ocean. Many SW sets can receive police, fire, and civil defense traffic. Listening in on rescue efforts such as the work of the Coast Guard along the Gulf coast during hurricane Camille (Fig. 1-7) is second only to being there in person. The "rag chewing" of radio hams (Fig. 1-8) situated all over the world can be relied on for an unending source of worthwhile technical and general comments.

To the rich and varied content of short-wave listening is added yet another exciting dimension—the realm of outer space. SWL'ers have discovered that over and beyond the earth's horizon, the void is being filled with radio signals from satellites and manned space capsules. Whether it's the "beep-beep" of a telemetry signal from a space probe or the

Fig. 1-6. A disaster brings into action two-way mobile radios that can be picked up by the SWL'er.

voice of an astronaut in orbit, many of these signals can be heard by the SWL'er at home on standard equipment. In fact, a considerable body of valuable tracking information has been provided to scientists through monitoring reports sent by SWL operators.

Fig. 1-7. Coast Guard rescue operation along Gulf coast during hurricane Camille. Communications could be monitored on short wave.

These are just samples of the exciting rewards waiting to be discovered on the short-wave bands. Acquiring them is not difficult; no license, electronic skill, or prohibitively expensive equipment is needed. But, as in any engaging and

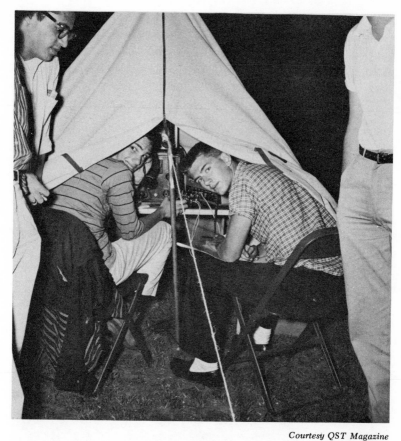

Fig. 1-8. The SWL'er can tune in on hundreds of ham stations, like this one, and listen to conversations from around the world.

lasting hobby, enjoyment grows with experience and knowledge. For the short-wave listener, this means acquiring familiarity with the behavior of short waves, receivers, antennas, tuning, program schedules, and a variety of other practical details, which we will explore next.

CHAPTER 2

The Short-Wave Signal

No one has ever seen a short-wave signal. It is an invisible field of energy that travels at the speed of light as it carries a program from the antenna of a station (Fig. 2-1) to the short-wave set. Yet, it is possible to describe and predict its behavior. In the process many terms that comprise the working vocabulary of the SWL'er begin to take on meaning. Words such as *wavelength, frequency, meter,* and even *short wave* itself can be understood and put to practical use. Let's begin by examining some of the basic features of radio waves—the raw material that makes up the very fabric of a short-wave signal.

The forces that produce a radio wave originate in the heart of the transmitter at the sending station. There, electrical currents are made to surge back and forth at extremely high speeds. As they progress through various stages in the transmitter, these alternating currents are boosted in power (Fig. 2-2) and finally applied to the transmitting tower. It is in

this area that currents give rise to the actual radio wave—
the field of energy that travels out from the tower.

A picture of the wave, as shown in Fig. 2-3, helps to ex-
plain some common terms used in short-wave listening. The
curve represents the strength and polarity (positive or negative) of the signal at a given instant. Since the wave that is
broadcast is generated by electrical currents in the antenna,

Courtesy Radiodiffusion-Télévision Francaise

Fig. 2-1. Transmitter facility of French broadcasting system at Allouis, France.

Fig. 2-2. Final stage of a transmitter producing 500 kilowatts of power.

it is similar. If the starting point of the curve is considered to be at the left, it is seen that the line starts from the zero point, rises, then returns to zero. This represents the part of the wave created when current in the tower is positive. As the same current reverses, so does the wave direction. This is shown by the line falling below the zero point. An excellent way to visualize the action is to compare it to the dropping of a pebble into a pond. Ripples are created that move in ever widening circles. Each wave of water has a peak (high point) that is followed by a dip (trough). These peaks and dips correspond to the positive and negative movements of the radio energy, as illustrated in Fig. 2-3.

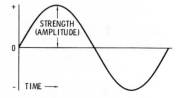

Fig. 2-3. One cycle of a wave.

There are several other important electronics terms used in short-wave radio. What has been shown in Fig. 2-3 is the radio wave going through one complete alternation (*cycle*). The number of cycles occurring each second determines the *frequency* of a wave. For example, a station in the standard (a-m) broadcast band might operate on a frequency which produces one million cycles every second.

Although "cycles per second" once served as the basic measure of frequency, it was supplanted in the 1960's by the term "hertz." The changeover honors Heinrich Hertz, a 19th-Century Austrian physicist who conducted early experiments with radio waves. Several abbreviations are employed to make the frequency less awkward to say and read. The prefix "kilo," meaning 1000, can be combined with hertz to form kilohertz (abbreviated kHz). One-million hertz thus becomes 1000 kHz. When frequencies run much higher, the prefix "mega"—for million—is often used. Our station could be correctly labelled also with the frequency "1 MHz" (1 megahertz).

The ability to convert kilohertz (kHz) to megahertz (MHz) is especially important for reading short-wave schedules. Station frequencies are given in either form. The dial of the SW receiver may be scaled with both systems. The rules are simple: anytime you wish to convert kilohertz to megahertz, move the decimal point three places to the left (for example, 2300 kHz = 2.3 MHz). Reversing the system, 6.2 MHz becomes 6200 kHz.

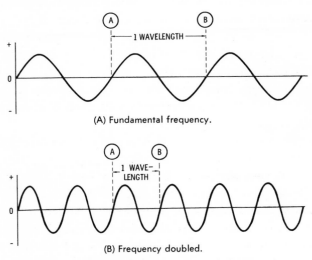

(A) Fundamental frequency.

(B) Frequency doubled.

Fig. 2-4. Doubling the frequency cuts the wavelength in half.

Another means of identifying a radio wave is in terms of wavelength. This is the distance from the beginning of one cycle to the beginning of the next as the waves radiate from the transmitting antenna. In the pebble and waterwave example, the wavelength is the number of inches or centimeters between each peak (crest). With radio energy the standard is the *meter* (one meter = 39.37 inches). Wavelength always varies with station frequency, as illustrated by Fig. 2-4.

Assume that the frequency of the wave in Fig. 2-4A is 15 MHz (15 million cycles occurring each second). Wavelength for this can be measured between points A and B. But suppose that the number of cycles per second were doubled (to 30 MHz), as in Fig. 2-4B. The important difference to observe is that a 30-MHz wave has two cycles for every one of the 15-MHz signal. In effect, the higher the frequency, the shorter the wavelength.

It is valuable to the short-wave listener to know how to convert frequency to wavelength. Although a specific station is always located on the dial by means of its exact frequency in kilohertz or megahertz, quite often wavelength (in meters) is used for general discussion. For example, the SWL'er might read reports about conditions on the 31-meter band. This is more convenient than singling out particular frequencies within that band (which lies between 9200 kHz and 9700 kHz). The characteristics of each of these closely spaced frequencies is quite uniform.

The formula for converting frequency to meters is:

$$\text{Wavelength (in meters)} = \frac{300,000,000}{\text{freq. (in hertz)}}$$

The 300,000,000 figure is always the same when the wavelength is in meters; it is the constant speed of all radio waves. (300,000,000 meters per second is the speed of light.) If you start with kilohertz or megahertz, the figure must be changed to hertz. As an example, what is the wavelength of a station operating on 30 MHz?

$$\text{Wavelength} = \frac{300,000,000}{30,000,000} = 10 \text{ meters}$$

As familiarity with the SW bands increases, you will have only occasional use for the formula. The major bands are soon memorized in terms of wavelength versus frequency. However, there is a mental shortcut which may be used. If one band is known, it's simple to approximate several others.

Anytime the frequency is cut in half, wavelength is doubled. In the above example, 30 MHz is equal to 10 meters; you would be correct in assuming 15 MHz is equal to 20 meters.

There is one instance when the formula is especially important: the design of special antennas which the SWL'er might wish to construct for reception exclusively on a particular band. As discussed in a later chapter, the formula yields the exact length of wire needed for the construction of such an antenna.

Table 2-1. The Radio Spectrum

Major Divisions	Frequency Ranges
VLF = Very Low Frequency	10 kHz to 30 kHz
LF = Low Frequency	30 kHz to 300 kHz
MF = Medium Frequency	300 kHz to 3000 kHz
HF* = High Frequency	3 MHz to 30 MHz
VHF = Very High Frequency	30 MHz to 300 MHz
UHF = Ultrahigh Frequency	300 MHz to 3000 MHz
SHF = Superhigh Frequency	3 GHz to 30 GHz
EHF = Extremely High Frequency	30 GHz to 300 GHz

* Most SW listening is done in this part of the spectrum.

Armed with the fundamental terms used in short wave, we can now consider the radio spectrum as a whole. It is a region that commences at the very-low frequency of approximately 10 kHz and extends upward and beyond 30,000 MHz. Other types of energy border the radio spectrum, but they are characterized by different properties. Light and X rays, for example, occupy the frequencies above the radio region. All short-wave listening is done on one or more of the eight major divisions shown in Table 2-1. By far the most popular classification is in the high-frequency (hf) range, from 3-30 MHz. As you will see in the next chapter, this is the area for long-distance broadcasting. To a lesser extent, there is activity of interest on the medium (mf) and very-high frequencies (vhf).

Finally, consider the definition of the word *short wave*. It may be a surprise to many, but the word itself is a living antique and survives by weight of tradition. It gives only a general description of a vague area in today's complex spectrum. In radio's earlier day, short wave meant anything above the standard broadcast band in the mf region. Since these waves were known to be high in frequency, it followed that wavelengths were short. Thus, the term short wave evolved. But a short-wave listener today might actually be an lf listener, if he has equipment that can tune to stations in the 200-kHz region. Wavelengths in this band are much longer than standard broadcast. But, in spite of its technical origin, short-wave listening is a durable and descriptive term for operations anywhere outside the standard bands of a-m, fm and tv.

CHAPTER 3

The Ionosphere

Without the ionosphere most short-wave listening would cease. It is this electrified layer of air extending about 60 to 250 miles above the earth's surface that reflects some radio waves back to earth (*skip*). This skip pathway carries radio signals between continents, over seas, and indeed, around the world. The ionosphere is not firmly fixed in place; constant shifts in position and thickness have a profound effect on radio waves. These and other factors determine whether a particular station can be received at a certain place at a given time. For this reason some knowledge of the ionosphere is of significant value to the short-wave listener.

The formation of the ionosphere is generally believed to be a result of the sun's action on the upper atmosphere. As huge amounts of ultraviolet radiation bombard gas molecules, an ionizing effect occurs; molecules are broken down into charged particles. The amount of ionization differs at varying heights, so a series of layers, which comprise the ionosphere as a whole, is created.

Since the sun has a direct effect on the ionosphere, the individual ionospheric layers are subject to great variation as the earth rotates. When the sun sets in a particular region, a reduction in ultraviolet radiation causes the ionosphere to thin out and move to greater heights. Seasons also alter the amount of radiation; they have an influence on the structure of the ionosphere, but over a longer period of time. Another major effect is caused by mysterious sunspots that appear to

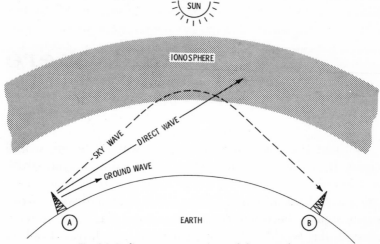

Fig. 3-1. Radio-wave propagation and the ionosphere.

cross the face of the sun in groups of varying size. When the average number of sunspots goes up, ultraviolet radiation rises with it. Thus, the most definite thing to be stated about radio conditions is that they change—hourly, with the seasons, and according to the sunspot cycle.

A basic view of ionospheric propagation is shown in Fig. 3-1. Depending on frequency, a radio wave may follow one of three principal paths as it travels away from the transmitting station (point A). For the lower end of the radio spectrum (below 3 MHz) the signal finds an excellent path along the surface of the earth. Although waves travel in straight lines, the conductivity of the ground tends to bend them so they curve over the horizon. This is known as ground-wave transmission. Since it does not depend on the shifting ionosphere, a ground-wave signal is quite reliable from year to year. Thus it is widely used for standard broadcast and certain radio beacon stations where permanent coverage is important. The chief limitation of the ground wave is range. Although signals follow the earth's curvature, they surrender energy to the ground in the process. Only in special applications is it worthwhile to transmit the enormous power required to propagate signals by means of the ground wave more than a few hundred miles. Another serious handicap is the amount of space available in the low-frequency portion of the spectrum. Only a limited number of stations can fit in the band where ground-wave transmission is favorable since the space is just a few megahertz wide.

Ignoring for a moment the 3- to 30-MHz region, consider vhf frequencies and the higher bands. Here the most significant path is the line-of-sight (*direct*) wave. As the wave leaves the antenna, it travels primarily between the tower and the ionosphere. Poor earth conductivity at these frequencies makes ground waves virtually nonexistent. Note in Fig. 3-1 that the direct wave penetrates the ionosphere with no apparent change in direction. This results because the ionosphere behaves differently toward different frequencies; as the frequency becomes higher (number of megahertz incrases), the ionized layers exert less of a bending influence. This accounts for the straight-line path of high frequencies. They are ultimately lost to space. Reception on vhf and upper bands occurs largely when both transmitting and receiving antennas can "see" each other. Note that the receiver (point B in Fig. 3-1) is too far below the horizon to pick up the direct wave from point A. For reception to occur, B would have to be moved closer to A, or, when practical, its antenna would have to be raised to intercept the wave.

Again we have a radio path that is not dependent on the ionosphere to any great extent, is also limited in range, but offers day-to-day reliability. Services which use direct-wave propagation include tv, fm broadcast, and various short-range and mobile operations. (There are notable exceptions to the range limitation in the over-30-MHz region. These are described later in the book.)

There is some short-wave listening via ground- and direct-wave paths, but the region from 3- to 30-MHz (hf) forms the heart of the SWL hobby. It is in this third category that the ionosphere produces the skip phenomenon. In Fig. 3-1 the sky wave is seen leaving transmitting antenna A and bouncing off the ionosphere. The reflected signal leaves the ionosphere at about the same angle as it enters, and receiver B intercepts the energy as the wave returns to earth. It is possible, too, for the wave at B to reflect from the earth's surface and repeat the identical process for a second skip (*multihop transmission*). Depending on a variety of conditions, great distances may be covered by a skip path. It is not uncommon for short-wave stations to broadcast to areas situated many thousands of miles distant from the transmitting tower.

Many variables must be taken into account in any attempt to predict the distance covered by the skip wave. One of them is frequency. As mentioned earlier, when the frequency of a signal increases, less ionospheric bending occurs. The principle is shown in Fig. 3-2 where all conditions are comparable except frequency.

In Fig. 3-2 the tower is radiating three signals: 7, 12, and 28 MHz. Notice that the relatively high 28-MHz signal follows a long sweeping arc through the ionosphere as it is bent. In fact, the resulting reflection is not sufficient to bring the signal back to earth; it shoots off into space. If the signal wave were steadily reduced in frequency, increased bending would ultimately bring it back to the earth's surface. This occurs at the *critical* frequency.

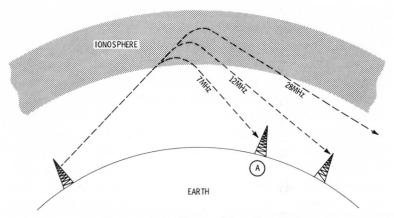

Fig. 3-2. Ionospheric effects on different frequencies.

The two remaining signals, 7 and 12 MHz, are well within the critical limits. They are shown returning to earth after a single skip. Note that 7 MHz covers a shorter distance (lower frequency means a sharper angle through the ionosphere). In this example, the 7-MHz signal would be called the maximum usable frequency for transmitting to point A. It is the highest frequency that can be used to strike that particular location.

For the sake of clarity, the three signals in Fig. 3-2 are shown leaving the transmitting tower at a rather high angle. In practical applications, however, long-distance stations generally design their antennas to keep the "angles of fire" as low as possible. When the radio wave is transmitted nearly parallel to the earth's surface, the total distance covered is at its greatest. Also, less bending in the ionosphere is needed to effect a return trip to earth.

The dynamic nature of the ionosphere causes considerable variation in the example. As mentioned earlier, the height of the layers changes with the sun's position. This influence also changes the reflection angles. In winter, for example, the shorter distance between the earth and sun produces greater concentrations of ultraviolet rays on the upper atmosphere. The ionosphere now becomes a thicker layer; its bending effect is more pronounced. One result is that winter can cause a return to earth of signals that are normally lost in space during summer. These are the frequencies that are above the critical limit in summer but angle down sufficiently during winter.

Sunspots working in approximately 11-year cycles, exercise a major influence on the variation in critical frequencies. As the number of sunspots rises, solar radiation climbs with it, and the ionosphere deepens. The net result is that during peaks in the sunspot cycle, higher frequencies are usable for long-distance skips. During dips in the cycle, the critical frequency hovers in the 20- to 30-MHz region.

The character of the ionosphere is still the subject of intense investigation. There are aspects of its behavior about which little is known. Massive disturbances occasionally occur during ionospheric storms that appear to originate during certain types of sunspot activity. These can absorb signals and virtually wipe out communications over a wide band for days at a time. Fast moving layers, known as sporadic-E ionization, appear intermittently in summer and open higher portions of the radio spectrum to an abnormal amount of skipping.

The variation of the ionosphere is no serious deterrent to the short-wave listener. Aided by the ample frequency coverage of the typical short-wave set as well as the large number of SW stations, some section of the spectrum is always open.

CHAPTER 4

The Short-Wave Receiver

As the major piece of equipment in the hobby of short-wave listening, the receiver must convert the minute energy of a radio wave into an audible signal. How well a receiver can do this is mostly a measure of its sensitivity and selectivity. The first quality, *sensitivity,* is the ability to separate a signal from the ever present noise level created by disturbances in the atmosphere and outer space.

Selectivity describes how well the receiver can pick out a signal in a crowded frequency band. It is mainly by these two qualities that a short-wave receiver may be judged. A multitude of features may appear in a given set, but these are usually concerned with operating convenience rather than operating quality.

BASIC RECEPTION

The sections shown in Fig. 4-1 make up the fundamental building blocks of the short-wave receiver. The first point encountered by radio waves is the *antenna*. Energy cuts across the wire and creates tiny electrical currents which surge up and down according to frequency. Since all waves in the immediate vicinity create antenna currents, it is the job of the *tuner* to select the desired wave. As the operator moves the receiver tuning dial, the circuit either accepts or rejects the incoming frequency.

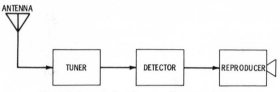

Fig. 4-1. Steps in hearing a radio transmission.

The signal emerging from the tuner is still radio-frequency energy. It is the job of the *detector* to recover the voice or music (*intelligence*) that has travelled atop the radio wave and to present it to the next stage—the reproducer. This may be earphones or a speaker, either of which is capable of changing audio frequencies (within the range of hearing) to audible sound waves.

With these basic concepts in mind, we can consider two major receiver types. The simpler of the two contains the regenerative circuit. Although it has certain limitations, it survives today because it has few parts and a low price. The circuit is illustrated in Fig. 4-2 in block-diagram form.

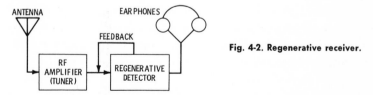

Fig. 4-2. Regenerative receiver.

As radio-frequency signals enter the rf amplifier, they are boosted in strength and applied to the regenerative detector. Not only is audio recovered from radio frequency, but an additional effect—regeneration—occurs in this stage. This is represented by an arrow marked "feedback." After the signal passes through the detector, a small portion of it is returned to the entry point. In effect, the stage is given another opportunity to boost—or amplify—the original signal. Audio currents emerge from the detector and drive the earphone.

Due to the feedback principle, the regenerative receiver displays a great deal of sensitivity with simple circuits. Its chief drawback is in the area of selectivity. As a signal becomes stronger in the regenerative set, it has the tendency to occupy a larger width on the tuning dial—a disadvantage under crowded conditions. It is often difficult, and sometimes impossible, to tune in a weak station that is close in frequency to a relatively strong one. Yet the regenerative circuit remains quite popular today as an inexpensive source for short-wave listening. If the selectivity loss is tolerated, the circuit will bring in a considerable number of distant stations. A typical set is shown in Fig. 4-3.

The *superheterodyne* receiver overcomes the disadvantages of the simpler regenerative set. Through a process of juggling frequencies the superhet can be tuned sharply to signals of virtually any strength. The operation is shown in Fig. 4-4. Antenna signals are first applied to the rf amplifier, where they are tuned, strengthened, and passed on to the mixer. Both the mixer and local oscillator work together to overcome a problem that exists in circuits operating at high frequencies. It is a general rule that the higher the operating frequency, the greater is the *bandwidth* of the receiver tuning circuits. This simply means that the receiver finds it more difficult to single out one station from a group if all stations occur high in the band.

Thus selectivity is poorer at 30 MHz, for example, than on 12 MHz. The mixer and local oscillator, however, correct this situation. No matter what the frequency of the received station, they convert it down to an extremely low value,

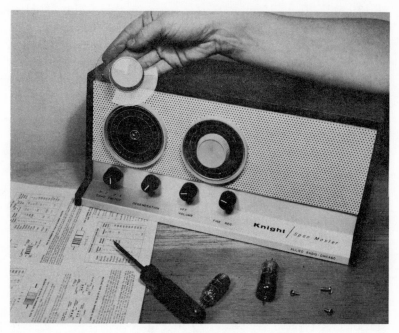

Fig. 4-3. Knight-Kit *Span Master* is an inexpensive regenerative set that can be assembled at home.

which is termed the *i-f frequency*. To illustrate how it is produced, assume that a short-wave station is transmitting on 12,200 kHz (12.2 MHz). The signal progresses through the rf amplifier and reaches the mixer; here, it encounters another signal (as shown by the arrow) that is produced by

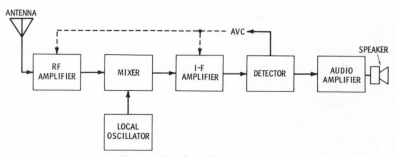

Fig. 4-4. Superheterodyne receiver.

the local oscillator. The oscillator behaves much like a miniature transmitter, generating a flow of radio-frequency current precisely at 12,655 kHz. The mixer stage is thereby provided with two signals: the original 12,200 kHz from the short-wave station, and the 12,655 kHz from the local oscillator.

Both frequencies proceed to mix in this stage, producing a difference of 455 kHz. This is the heterodyne principle— a mixing together of two signals produces a third frequency. A familiar example of the idea occurs when two original tones heard, but a "sour" sound is also created. It is the result of tones mixing and establishing a "beat" note that upsets the normally pleasant sound of the piano. The beat signal in the receiver, however, achieves the desirable result of transforming the original station frequency down to the very low value of 455 kHz. In this region, tuning circuits are quite sharp and selective.

How the local oscillator consistently produces the proper mixing frequency is determined by the tuning dial of the receiver. As the operator selects a station, the dial not only varies tuning of the rf amplifier; it controls the local oscillator as well. No matter what the incoming station frequency, the oscillator will produce a signal 455 kHz higher. When the receiver is tuned to 3,000 kHz, for example, the oscillator automatically generates 3,455 kHz.

Next in the chain is the i-f amplifier. This is a stage which accepts the signal (now 455 kHz) and boosts its strength. It does this in a highly efficient manner. Unlike the rf amplifier which must tune over a large range of frequencies, the i-f amplifier operates solely on 455 kHz. This single-channel nature permits excellent efficiency.

The detector and audio amplifier complete the receiving process. Here the signal is converted to audio-frequency energy and finally amplified for driving the speaker.

An additional circuit in the superhet receiver, shown as avc in the diagram, aids in the control of sensitivity. It is entirely possible for an incoming station to be so strong that it overloads the rf and i-f stages, causing mushy sound in the speaker. This is corrected by the automatic-volume-control (avc) voltage from the detector. As the signal grows stronger, the avc voltage increases. When fed back to the rf and i-f stages, it reduces their ability to amplify. Overall action is smooth and continuous to keep the sensitivity of the receiver within the proper limits. When extremely weak signals are being received, avc virtually disappears, and the circuits are allowed to run wide open.

RECEIVER CONTROLS

The number of knobs, switches, and dials on the front panel of a short-wave receiver is subject to much variation. In Fig. 4-5, for example, an elaborate set with more than a dozen individual elements to be tuned, adjusted, or observed is shown. With some experience, the infinite number of possible dial combinations can help strip a weak signal of noise, thus making it perfectly clear for listening.

Consider each major element which might appear on the front panel of a typical superhet SW receiver (Fig. 4-6). On the large rectangular dial there are four major divisions,

Fig. 4-5. Hallicrafters *Model SX-122A* short-wave receiver.

marked A,B,C, and D. These represent the four bands, encompassing the total frequency coverage of the set. Closer inspection reveals that it starts at 550 kHz near *A* and terminates at 30 MHz on band D. This indicates that the receiver is capable of an overall range of 550 kHz to 30 MHz, the coverage typical of most SW sets. Band A is devoted to standard a-m broadcast, a factor which increases the utility value of the receiver. The first SW band starts at *B* with 1.6 MHz, immediately above the broadcast band. When considering any short-wave receiver, be certain that the

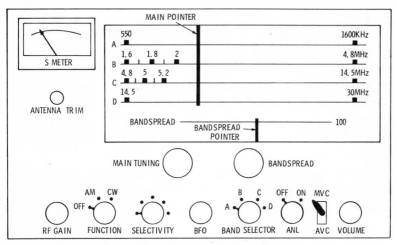

Fig. 4-6. Typical front-panel receiver controls.

bands run continuously with no gaps in the coverage. Many SW-receiver manufacturers make amateur-radio receivers that look quite similar to their short-wave models. If these units are limited to ham bands only, they will not provide the necessary short-wave coverage. Just be certain that each band progresses to the next with an uninterrupted rise in frequency. (There are general-coverage receivers, however, that may be operated on both ham and SW.)

The calibration of a typical band is shown on band B. Beginning with 1.6 MHz, each division increases the frequency by 0.1 MHz (100 kHz), a spacing which may not be the same for higher bands.

Assume that you wish to tune in a station on 5100 kHz (5.1 MHz). The set is first turned on by moving the function selector from Off to AM. (All SW-broadcast stations transmitting music and voice use a-m—amplitude modulation.) Then, the Band Selector is clicked to the appropriate band, C in this case. Note that there are two tuning knobs to select the frequency, Main Tuning and Bandspread. Before touching the Main Tuning control, the Bandspread is always preset to the end of its scale recommended by the manufacturer. Unless this step is done, the frequency shown on the dial face will not be correct. Now the Main Tuning dial is manipulated to bring the large pointer to the division between 5.0 and 5.2 MHz. If the desired frequency does not fall exactly on a dial calibration, the operator must do some estimating. For example, on 5,150 kHz the pointer would be centered in the space between 5.1 and 5.2 MHz. (Note that 5.1 MHz is not marked as such but is represented by a small division on the scale.)

The purpose of the Bandspread dial is to provide a means of fine tuning. It gives the effect of expanding a small portion of a band to make station location easier. Main Tuning, which moves rapidly across the band, is most useful for locating a particular segment of a band, while Bandspread can quickly pick out a particular frequency. For many SW receivers the Bandspread scale is marked in arbitrary numbers, not representing actual frequencies but rather dial-pointer positions. As the Bandspread pointer is moved from 100 toward zero, it lowers the frequency of the receiver by several hundred kilohertz. This suggests a second method for station location. Main Tuning is set on 5200 kHz and Bandspread on 100. Then Bandspread is slowly rotated toward zero until the desired station on 5150 kHz is heard. For future reference both Main Tuning and Bandspread numbers may be noted so the station can be quickly relocated.

The action of the S Meter furnishes valuable information about signal conditions. An actual meter on a set is shown in Fig. 4-7. As the receiver is tuned, the needle will rise and fall with signal strength. Thus, the meter is a helpful tuning aid. The Bandspread can be carefully adjusted for the highest meter reading on a particular station. When conditions are unstable, the needle will swing intermittently downward

Fig. 4-7. S meter on Hammarlund **HQ-180AC** receiver.

each time the signal fades. Heavy atmospheric noise also registers on the meter, revealing at a glance the natural noise level in relation to station strength. The S Meter is also useful for giving signal reports to SW stations. The meter face is marked off in universally understood S units and decibels.

Other dials on the front panel allow a number of adjustments for improving reception. The antenna trimmer (ANT. TRIM.), under the S Meter in this example, helps to match the antenna to the first tuning circuit in the set. In operation, it is rotated until the S Meter indicates a high reading for a given station. The setting remains the same over a given portion of a band but should be touched up for each station tuned. When ignition or atmospheric noises are high, they can be reduced by turning on the automatic noise limiter (ANL).

Problems of noise and interference are the province of the Selectivity control, usually found only on the more expensive receiver. It is generally a multiposition switch that adjusts the bandwidth of the receiver from broad to narrow. However, the choice of selectivity is not always a simple one. As the switch is advanced toward the narrow limit, the quality of sound from the speaker begins to deteriorate. The greatest naturalness in tone, especially important when receiving music, occurs in the broadest selectivity position. However, interference located a few kilohertz from the station frequency can make listening impossible. An increase in selectivity by one or two switch positions can usually reject the interfering signal, if the poorer audio quality is acceptable. This problem is far less important on voice. Since the requirement for voice is intelligibility rather than pleasing tones, the receiver can be narrowed considerably to eliminate interference. Maximum selectivity, however, is not preferred, since the higher voice tones are sliced off, and the words become increasingly difficult to understand. The sharpest selectivity is normally reserved for code reception where signals are extremely narrow. It should be noted that as receiver selectivity is increased, the amount of noise picked up is lessened. Again, the operator must choose the amount of selectivity according to the existing conditions.

The remaining controls are chiefly for code reception and thus are valuable only if the SWL'er intends to learn International Morse Code in preparation for a ham radio license. To set up the receiver for this type of reception, the Function Selector is turned to CW (continuous wave). This energizes a circuit in the set which supplies the necessary tone. The BFO (beat-frequency oscillator) control enables the code tone to be varied for the most pleasing sound. Neither the S meter nor the avc can follow the rapid fluctuations of a code signal. The AVC-MVC switch is placed on MVC (manual-volume control). This disables the meter and brings into play the RF Gain control. If a cw signal overloads the receiver, rf gain is varied manually to reduce the amplification.

(A) Inserting components into board.

(B) Assembling completed boards.

Fig. 4-8. Putting together a short-wave—receiver kit.

The receiver just described is not an actual set, but it does typify the type of equipment the SWL'er is likely to encounter. The placement of knobs and dials is by no means standard; it is apt to vary from one model to the next. Yet their basic functions remain the same. How well the receiver performs is also subject to considerable variation. Two different receivers may have similar controls marked "Selectivity," but this is not a guide to the effectiveness of the circuits behind the panel. As with most electronic equipment, the reputable manufacturer offers improved circuit quality and performance with price.

Building your own receiver from a kit is a popular way of acquiring a better set than might be available for the same cost in a factory-assembled unit. Fig. 4-8 shows a set under construction that is equipped with many desirable features. The completed receiver is pictured in Fig. 6-5.

Fig. 4-9. Zenith *Model Royal 7000.*

One of the most advanced receivers available is shown in Fig. 4-9. Its eleven bands include: vhf/fm weather band; long-wave weather stations; navigation band; five international short-wave bands; fm and am broadcast bands; and others.

CHAPTER 5

Antennas

Following the receiver, the next most important piece of short-wave equipment is the antenna. It is the job of the "skyhook" to intercept radio waves in the immediate vicinity and convert them into currents to be delivered to the receiver. Most SW sets pick up some distant stations with a short length of wire attached to the antenna terminal. However, the number of signals is increased remarkably with an efficient antenna "high and in the clear."

It is appropriate to consider an antenna as a system comprising three elements: antenna, transmission line (popularly called the lead-in), and ground (Fig. 5-1). The antenna proper is the section that performs the actual signal pickup. To this end, it is mounted as high as possible. Be certain that it is free of nearby obstructions that may block the waves. Coupled to the antenna is the transmission line for carrying the signal down to the antenna terminals of the receiver. The remaining element is the ground which helps to complete the signal pathway and affords some degree of protection from lightning. (A lightning arrestor must be used on the lead-in wire, however.) Practical short-wave antennas often combine one or more of these elements; for example, antenna and transmission line may be a single, uninterrupted run of wire.

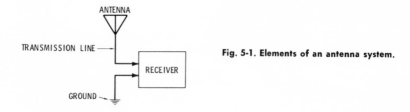

Fig. 5-1. Elements of an antenna system.

In selecting from among the various antenna types, the SWL'er must compromise in antenna length. Any piece of wire behaves like a tuned circuit to radio waves; as it is made shorter, it tends to favor higher frequencies. Thus, a dilemma develops in the attempt to choose a single length to operate efficiently over the wide frequency spectrum of the short-wave bands. An antenna on 3 MHz, for example, performs best when it is about 150 feet long, while a 15-foot wire best serves 30 MHz reception. It is impractical to erect a mulitude of antennas to cover all frequency groups, but there are workable techniques. With the high sensitivity of today's short-wave receiver, a single compromise antenna—the inverted L—is quite adequate for most listening. As the SWL'er advances in his hobby, he may resort to a more specialized antenna (detailed later) to improve sensitivity in a particular band or groups of bands.

INVERTED L

The inverted L is the simplest and most common SW antenna, deriving its name from a resemblance to the letter L placed upside down (Fig. 5-2A). Overall length of the wire is 40 to 100 feet, and there is no distinct transmission line

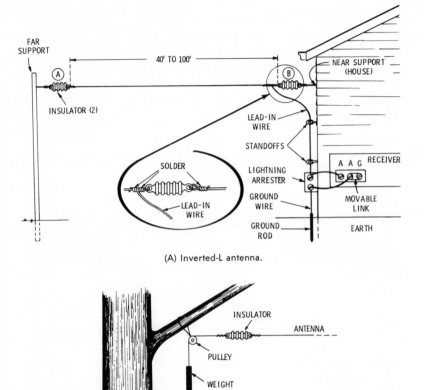

(A) Inverted-L antenna.

(B) Pulley and weight arrangement.

Fig. 5-2. Details of an antenna system.

other than the antenna wire itself. Depending on available space, the antenna should run as long and as straight as possible to the far support.

Consider a step-by-step procedure for installing an inverted L. It is best to begin by figuring out the most convenient location for the far support. This may be a nearby pole, house, or garage roof. A tree is a definite possibility if it is fairly rigid; sway is likely to snap the wire. If this type

45

of support is used, try to select a tree with a relatively thick trunk. It is feasible to use a thin tree if some method of allowing for movement is devised. The system shown in Fig. 5-2B is one suggestion. In any case the far support should permit maximum antenna height—30 feet or more off the ground, if possible. Next, determine the distance from far to near supports plus the length required for the lead-in part of the antenna. The total will be the amount of wire needed for the job. Don't forget to allow extra footage for inside the house.

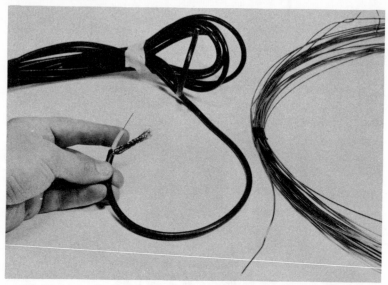

Fig. 5-3. Large roll of wire is hard-drawn copper, and the other is coaxial cable.

Almost any type of wire can serve for the antenna as long as it will not sag over a period of time. The heat of summer can cause considerable expansion of the wire. Also, the formation of ice in the winter can lower the original height. A good choice of wire is No. 12 or 14 hard-drawn copper, as shown in Fig. 5-3. It does not matter whether the wire is coated with enamel or other kind of insulation. The only place bare metal must show is at the hookup point at the receiver antenna terminals and the solder points shown in Fig. 5-2B. (Another good wire choice is copper-clad steel.)

The installation job is made easier if most assembly work is done before the antenna is erected. While it is on the ground insulators at points A and B may be fastened to the ends of the antenna wire (Fig. 5-2). The insulators may be porcelain or glass of the 3- or 4-inch size (Fig. 5-4). Solder

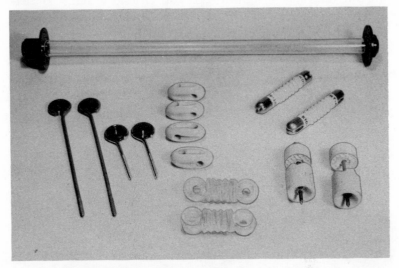

Fig. 5-4. Suggested hardware for stringing a short-wave antenna.

the lead-in section of the wire and bring it down the side of the house through insulated stand-offs. The screw-in type used for TV twin lead can serve well in this case. The antenna loses the least signal if contact with any surface is avoided as it runs down the side of the house—this also includes the entry point. (A lightning arrester, Fig. 5-5, is recommended at the entry point.)

When the antenna is actually raised, extreme caution must be used. The wire should never be allowed to touch, or even pass close to, power lines. Not only is this in the interest of safety, but noise interference generated by the power line is reduced. Final attachment of the insulators to the far and near supports may be done with appropriate lengths of the same wire used for the antenna.

A good ground is essential for the lightning arrester to properly drain off electrical charges that occur during a thunderstorm. (Sparking and possible damage to the tuning section of the receiver can occur even though the antenna is not hit directly by lightning.) The ground system consists of a heavy bare wire run to a pipe driven into the earth. (Both of these items are commonly available where TV parts are sold.) The same ground may be used to hook the receiver ground terminal to earth.

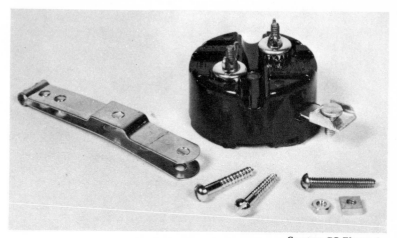

Courtesy GC Electronics

Fig. 5-5. Universal lightning arrester.

In the case of the apartment dweller, the ground system outlined may be impractical. The alternative is to connect to the electrical ground of the building. This may be done at a cold-water pipe or the screw that holds the cover plate on an ac wall outlet. (In no instance should a gas pipe be used for a ground.) Special grounding clamps (Fig. 5-6) are sold for providing good contact with a pipe.

There is an important consideration when grounding an ac-dc short-wave set. It could be hazardous to ground any of the screws used to hold the cabinet or chassis in place. Just be certain to follow the manufacturer's recommendations, which usually indicate that only the terminal marked G or GND be used for grounding.

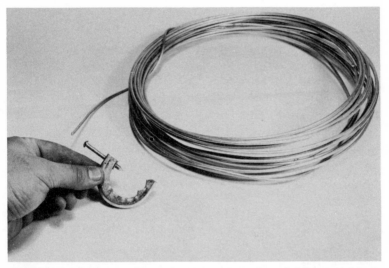

Fig. 5-6. Special clamp and heavy aluminum wire recommended for ground leads.

The completed inverted-L antenna displays some directionality; that is, it favors signals arriving from certain directions. Since different frequencies react to antenna lengths in varying manners, it is difficult to predict the pattern of response. Generally, the antenna tends to favor those signals which arrive broadside to its length. Thus, signals from east and west might be heard more strongly in an antenna that lies in a north-south direction. The directional problem is not usually serious, but some experimentation might prove worthwhile. If space permits, a new far support might be located and the direction of the antenna changed for improved results.

The other two antennas to be described are of interest to the more advanced listener who is willing to sacrifice the broad response of the inverted L in favor of improved performance on a narrower range of frequencies. The same basic constructional techniques apply as before. Maximum height assures good signal pickup and a reduction in noise from man-made sources such as motors, power lines, and automobile ignition.

FOLDED DIPOLE

The folded dipole works best for single-band operation. It is constructed with TV-type twin-lead wire rated at 300 ohms (Fig. 5-7). The length of the top part of the wire determines the operating frequency. (The lead-in or transmission-line section may be any length in all cases.) Finding the correct length for any particular frequency is done with the aid of a simple formula:

$$\text{Length in feet} = \frac{468}{\text{frequency in MHz}}$$

To illustrate the use of the formula, assume you wanted to cut the antenna for the 31-meter band which extends from 9200 to 9700 kHz. First, the center of the band, which is

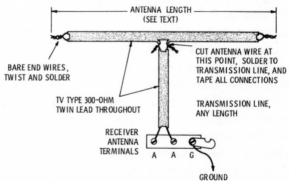

Fig. 5-7. Folded-dipole antenna.

9450 kHz, is converted to megahertz (9.45 MHz). Inserted into the formula:

$$\text{Length in feet} = \frac{468}{9.45}$$

The answer is approximately 49 feet. This is the dimension indicated as antenna length in Fig. 5-7. The transmission line is joined to the exact center of this length, as shown.

A folded dipole of this size will work well over the complete 31-meter band. It is quite directional and should be oriented so its length is run at right angles to the stations you wish to favor. Thus, an SWL'er in Chicago might run a folded dipole along a north-south line and achieve greatest sensitivity to stations from Europe to the east and the Orient to the west.

The folded dipole nets a specific advantage over the inverted L. Since the twin-lead running from the antenna to the receiver is a true transmission line, it has the ability to cancel some of the noise originating below the antenna proper. This is not true of the inverted L, which is indiscriminately sensitive over its total length. But again it should be emphasized that the folded dipole attenuates (weakens) signals outside the band for which it is cut.

Connecting the folded dipole to the receiver differs from the method of attaching the inverted L. As shown in Fig. 5-2A, there are three terminals on the typical SW receiver —two marked A and one marked G. For the inverted L connection, a movable link is fastened across A and G, and the wire is hooked as illustrated. With the folded dipole, there are two leads from the transmission line and these go to A and A (Fig. 5-7). There is a simple trick for converting the folded dipole to a single-wire antenna that resembles the inverted L in performance. The two wires at the bottom end of the twin lead can be twisted together and hooked to the receiver terminals in the same fashion as the inverted-L antenna.

FAN DIPOLE

Although it is physically the most complex of the three antennas described here, the fan dipole is capable of good response over an approximate range of 6 to 18 MHz. It requires a support about 30 feet high and a transmission line of 50-ohm coaxial line. The dimensions are given in Fig. 5-8. In order for the antenna to perform well, the shield of the

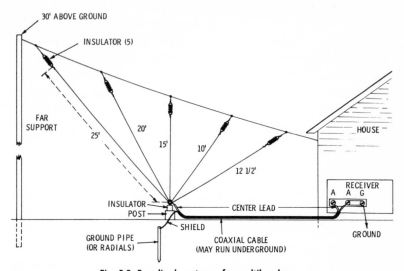

Fig. 5-8. Fan-dipole antenna for multiband use.

coaxial cable should be properly grounded at the base of the antenna where the leads merge. If the soil is normally moist, a simple ground rod driven to a depth of about 4 feet will suffice. In sandy areas where earth conductivity is likely to be poor, four or five lengths of bare copper wire should be buried in the ground and attached to the coaxial shield. These wires (called radials) can lie a few inches below ground and should extend outward from the antenna base in different directions. The fan dipole is a vertical antenna and picks up signals from all directions with fairly equal sensitivity.

CHAPTER 6

How To Set Up and Operate Your Set

A short-wave receiver may be operated virtually any-where—on a kitchen tabletop or in an elaborate fully equipped "shack." However, several considerations should be taken into account before choosing a particular location. You'll need room for the addition of accessories, wall space for charts, and a drawer or shelf for various papers.

The neatest installation can be made by placing the receiver close to an ac outlet and near the window where the antenna enters. Such a position reduces the number of trailing wires and makes the antenna more efficient by keeping the transmission line short. If this area happens to be in a living room, where other members of the family tend to congregate, remember that they may not be as fascinated as you are with short-wave listening—they may even find sounds from the speaker objectionable or in conflict with a nearby TV set. This problem can generally be eliminated by using earphones. With most SW receivers, the plugging in of earphones automatically quiets the speaker. But there is a disadvantage; earphone listening can become tiring after a while. The earphones are most valuable during late night hours when sounds from the set are apt to be objectionable anywhere in the house.

A basic SW setup is shown in Fig. 6-1. Notice that the receiver is not placed directly on top of the table; instead it rests on a shallow shelf. Two purposes are served by the

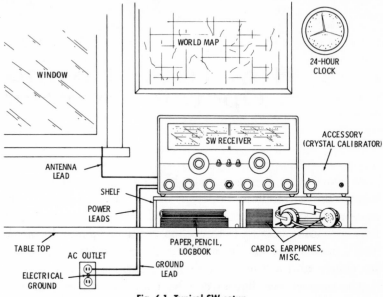

Fig. 6-1. Typical SW setup.

shelf: it is easier to operate controls on the receiver if they are raised several inches above the surface of the table, and the dial face is closer to eye level so that the small numbers and divisions are easier to read. The best receiver position is one in which the top edge of the cabinet is slightly tilted away from the eye of the listener. This places the dial directly in line of vision. It provides the same effect as bending your head down to the dial and looking directly at it.

These considerations may seem minor at first, but they do pay off handsomely over hours of operating.

The supporting shelf for the receiver makes a fine receptacle (or "cubby hole") for storing such assorted necessities as blank paper, schedules, cards, and log books. As shown in the illustration, the shelf is extended to the right to accommodate those accessories which the SWL'er may wish to acquire. The wall above the operating table has ample room for charts of the world and a 24-hour world clock.

CALIBRATION

Although it is possible to search across the SW bands and discover interesting stations by accident, it is a definite advantage to know how to calibrate the dial accurately. Most short-wave dials are simply not accurate enough to be used as an absolute guide to frequency. Some kind of dependable reference signal is necessary to correct for error or unmarked frequency divisions. Whichever method you choose, the receiver should be permitted to warm up for at least a half hour in advance. This allows all circuits to reach proper operating temperature and cuts down the amount of drifting. Otherwise you are likely to calibrate the receiver and find that readings have shifted due to heating. That extra half hour of operation need not alarm anyone about the cost of electricity. A typical SW set, operated on the average ac line, may run five hours on a penny! As for wearing out the set, there is no problem here, either. If the ventilation holes on the cabinet are not blocked, preventing air circulation, there are no harmful effects. (Most receiver wear actually occurs because of the surge of electricity when the set is turned on.)

One simple method of calibration is with known stations. After some experience is gained on the bands, certain strong stations are readily located. If their announced frequencies are noted, it is a simple matter to use them for future reference. Assume that a known station is on 9120 kHz, but your dial incorrectly indicates 9240 kHz when that station is tuned in. The dial error therefore is +120 kHz. This error will probably hold true for several hundred kilohertz above and below the known frequency. Thus, if you wished to find a station on 8870 kHz, you would first set the dial pointer on this frequency and then move it *up* 120 kHz to allow for the error. It is possible to "spot" comparable points in other bands with several known stations for other calibration markers.

Of great value to the SWL'er is the service provided by the National Bureau of Standards, a branch of the U.S. Government. This agency operates powerful stations in Colorado and Hawaii that transmit signals of extremely high accuracy throughout the radio spectrum. Not only do they provide calibration points, but time signals as well. These stations are readily identified by the sound of a tone and ticking, plus voice announcements according to the schedule given in Table 6-1.

The most efficient means available to the SWL'er for pinpointing frequency is the crystal calibrator. This is an accessory which generates a series of accurate and closely

Table 6-1. Standard Frequency Stations and Propagation Reports

Station	Frequency (MHz)	Location
WWV*	2.5, 5, 10, 15, 20, 25	Fort Collins, Colorado
WWVH	2.5, 5, 10, 15	Maui, Hawaii
CHU	3.330, 7.335, 14.76	Ottawa, Canada
JJY	2.5, 4, 5, 8, 10, 15	Tokyo, Japan

* Propagation reports for the North Atlantic area are broadcast every five minutes following the station call letters. They consist of a letter indicating current conditions and a number indicating the forecast for the next six hours. Coding is:

W (· − −) = Disturbed
U (· · −) = Unsettled
N (− ·) = Normal

1. (· − − − −) Useless
2. (· · − − −) Very poor
3. (· · · − −) Poor
4. (· · · · −) Fair to Poor
5. (· · · · ·) Fair
6. (− · · · ·) Fair to Good
7. (− − · · ·) Good
8. (− − − · ·) Very Good
9. (− − − − ·) Excellent

spaced signals through the complete range of the SW receiver. These signals are heard as a tone when the BFO, or CW oscillator, on the receiver is turned on. The device is available in a transistorized version which needs no power source other than its own internal battery. On the lower bands, the calibrator radiates enough signals so that no connection into the receiver is required. For higher ranges, a connection to the antenna terminal may be needed.

The SWL'er is confronted with calibrators available in a number of price brackets. Inexpensive units can be purchased in kit form to be assembled by the owner. Small transistor units containing integrated circuits are popular. Several companies offer more elaborate calibrators that contain amplifiers so the output is stronger at the higher frequencies.

A typical calibrator contains a single crystal that produces an accurate signal every 100 kHz on the receiver dial up to about 50 MHz. Better units contain amplifiers so the calibrating signal is strong enough to use in the gigahertz region. Nearly all contain a trimmer adjustment for zeroing crystals precisely to the accurate signals transmitted by frequency-standard stations such as WWV. The crystal calibrator shown in Fig. 6-2 is typical of the ones currently available.

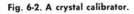

Fig. 6-2. A crystal calibrator.

Courtesy R. L. Drake Co.

TIME CONVERSION

Many short-wave schedules are conveniently printed in the listener's local time. For example, an SWL'er on the west coast of the U.S.A. might note that a program from Radio Sweden will be aired at 8:00 A.M., Pacific Standard Time (PST). No calculations are required—the listener simply looks at his own clock and tunes in at the appointed hour. Of course, it is not 8 A.M. in Sweden at the time of the broadcast. To prevent confusion over the different time zones throughout the world, a standard system has been universally adopted. It is GMT—Greenwich Mean Time. In many instances a program schedule is expressed entirely in

Table 6-2. Conventional Time Versus 24-Hour Time

Conventional Clock	24-Hour Clock
12 Midnight	0000
1 AM	0100
2 AM	0200
3 AM	0300
4 AM	0400
5 AM	0500
6 AM	0600
7 AM	0700
8 AM	0800
9 AM	0900
10 AM	1000
11 AM	1100
12 Noon	1200
1 PM	1300
2 PM	1400
3 PM	1500
4 PM	1600
5 PM	1700
6 PM	1800
7 PM	1900
8 PM	2000
9 PM	2100
10 PM	2200
11 PM	2300

GMT, requiring that the listener figure out what it means in terms of local time. Converting GMT to local time is not a difficult calculation and should be a permanent part of the short-wave listener's basic technique.

The idea behind GMT is the use of a single point in the world that stations and listeners alike agree on as a reference. Down through the years the Greenwich observatory, located on the south coast of England, has served this purpose. Another aspect of GMT is that time is based on a 24-hour world clock, as opposed to the more familiar 12-hour type. This further prevents confusion by eliminating the possibility of 8 o'clock meaning either a morning or an evening hour. Table 6-2 gives the 24-hour equivalents of conventional time. Note that 2030 hours, for example, would mean 8:30 P.M.

Assume a schedule states that a program is to be aired at 1300 GMT. If you consult Table 6-3, it will be seen that various time zones in the U.S.A. lag behind GMT by a certain number of hours. For those located in the Eastern Time belt, the number "−5" applies. This means that you should deduct 5 hours from GMT; the answer is local time for that area. Thus, a program aired at 1300 GMT will be picked up at 0800 EST, or 8 o'clock in the morning. Let's say a listener in the midwest wishes to hear a program scheduled for 0200 GMT. Applying the "−6" shown for the Central Standard Time zone, the answer is 2000 hours local (or CST) time. This is 8 o'clock in the evening.

Table 6-3. Converting GMT to Local Time*

Local Time	GMT	Local Time	GMT
Atlantic Standard Time	−4	Yukon Standard Time	− 9
Eastern Standard Time	−5	Alaska Standard Time	−10
Central Standard Time	−6	Bering Standard Time	−11
Mountain Standard Time	−7	Hawaii Standard Time	−10
Pacific Standard Time	−8		

* Add 1 hour to final answer for Daylight Saving Time.

A handy accessory which automatically figures out these time relationships is the 24-hour clock. The model shown in Fig. 6-3 tells GMT and local time (anywhere in the world) at a glance.

Assume that the clock is used in the vicinity of New York City and that local time is 15 minutes past 11 in the evening. The hour hand, as illustrated, points nearly straight up at 23 (2300 hours) and the minute hand is on the 15 minute mark at the right. Notice that the light-colored disc on the clock is actually a map of the world projected from the South Pole. To find GMT, it is only necessary to find "London-GMT" printed on the edge of the disc and read the time indicated at this point. In this example it is just above the

Fig. 6-3. A 24-hour world clock.

Fig. 6-4. Zenith's *Trans-Oceanic* portable.

minute hand and occupies the 0400 position (shown as "4"). Thus, 2315 EST (New York time) is the same as 0415 GMT. The whole map rotates continuously with the hour hand, and all time zones shift simultaneously. The time in other world locations on the map may also be checked with this system.

The only precaution in using Table 6-3 or the clock just described occurs in the areas of the U.S.A. which use Daylight Saving time during the summer months. Since all the figures are true for standard time only, a 1-hour adjustment must be made. Always add an hour to the final figure whenever calculations are made in a Daylight Saving time period. (The same precaution applies when using receivers which have built in devices for calculating time, as shown in Fig. 6-4.)

These are the basic tools of the SWL'er. Handling of receiver controls is best learned by actual experience rather than through a detailed description given here. However, there are two general recommendations in operating technique that should prove to be helpful. Most important, tuning should be done gingerly and with extreme care. The short-wave bands are often quite crowded, and hasty dial twisting can cause you to overlook much of the interesting material being broadcast. Finally, don't hesitate to experiment with different control settings. A change in selectivity here, or a touch up of the antenna trimmer there, will often salvage what sounds like a hopelessly weak station and render it perfectly readable.

Fig. 6-5. Heathkit *Model GR-78* is a battery-operated general coverage receiver.

All short-wave listening is by no means restricted to the elaborate setup just described. With the emergence of the transistor, portables similar to the one shown in Fig. 6-5 enable the hobbyist to carry on his activities anywhere. Requiring little battery power, these sets have coverage on the major SW bands and perform well under favorable conditions. The model illustrated in Fig. 6-5 uses 11 bipolar and 5 field-effect transistors in its circuitry. It can be operated from self-contained nickel-cadmium batteries. A built-in battery charger operates when the set is connected to an ac outlet. This portable may also serve as a first ham receiver. Although frequency coverage is continuous through all short-wave bands, major ham bands are directly calibrated on the bandspread tuning dial.

CHAPTER 7

Chasing DX

Listening to the world's short-wave stations requires some electronic detective work. It is true that some activity always prevails on the bands, but much of the choice listening requires careful preparation. There are program schedules to be studied, propagation reports to be analyzed, and logs to be written up and consulted. These are the tactics needed to unearth DX (the general term applied to distant stations). Chasing DX presents an interesting challenge to the SWL'er, especially in the face of changing conditions.

SHORT-WAVE BROADCAST BANDS

Most countries of the world meet periodically to agree on how to utilize the hundreds of frequencies available for international broadcasting. The frequencies are not scattered throughout the radio spectrum in random fashion, but assembled into groupings known as *bands*. It is customary to identify each band in terms of the approximate length of radio waves that fall within the band, expressed in meters. (A meter is 39.37 inches long.) Wavelength varies with frequency; the higher the frequency, the shorter the wavelength. How the major short-wave bands are arranged by meters is shown in Table 7-1. Although listening is not restricted solely to this part of the radio spectrum, these bands remain the chief hunting ground for DX.

Table 7-1. International Short-Wave Broadcast Bands

Meters	Frequency Range (kHz)
60	4750 to 5060
49	5950 to 6200
41	7100 to 7300
31	9500 to 9775
25	11,700 to 11,975
19	15,100 to 15,450
16	17,700 to 17,900
13	21,450 to 21,750
11	25,600 to 26,100

A representative schedule of stations and frequencies heard on the North American continent is given in Table 7-2. The frequencies shown are not necessarily constant; in some cases, stations shift channels according to propagation conditions.

60-Meter Band

Programming on the 60-meter band is primarily domestic; that is, the stations are broadcasting to local listeners. However, it is often possible to receive such signals at considerable distances. The 60-meter region is designated the "tropical band" since many of the stations are situated in South and Central America. Occasionally the central and southern parts of Africa are also heard.

Reception on the band is usually most favorable during winter months in the early evening.

Table 7-2. A Schedule of Stations and Frequencies

Frequency (kHz)	Identification	Location
3265	Radio Tamandare	Recife, Brazil
3295	Radio Cultura de Serguipe	Aracaju, Brazil
3322	Radio Bougainville	Kieta, Bougainville
3350	Radio Ghana	Accra, Ghana
3385	Radio Rabaul	Rabaul, New Britain Is.
4723	Burmese Broadcasting Service	Rangoon, Burma
4760	Radio Tingo Maria	Tingo Maria, Peru
4834	Radio Mali	Bamako, Mali
4835	Radio Malaysia Sarawak	Kuching, Sarawak
4545	Radio San Isidro	La Ceiba, Honduras
4885	Radio Universo	Barquisimeto, Venezuela
4890	Voice of Kenya	Nairobi, Kenya
4920	Australian Broadcasting Comm.	Brisbane, Australia
4940	Radio Kiev	Kiev, USSR
5070	Radio Nacional	Mazatenango, Guatemala
5965	Radio Guaiba	Porto Alegre, Brazil
5980	Radio Demerara	Georgetown, Guyana
5990	Radio Sweden	Stockholm, Sweden
6005	Radio Progreso	La Paz, Bolivia
6010	Cape Breton Broadcasting Corp.	Sydney, N.S., Canada
6025	Radio Portugal	Lisbon, Portugal
6030	Voice of the Prairies	Calgary, Alta., Canada
6055	Radio Mexico	Mexico City, Mexico
6095	Radio Baghdad	Baghdad, Iraq
6110	British Broadcasting Corp	London, England
6125	Radio TV Belge	Brussels, Belgium
6140	Radio Nacional de Espana	Madrid, Spain
6145	Radio Biafra	Orlu, Biafra
6160	Canadian Broadcasting Corp.	St. Johns, Newf., Canada
6165	Radio Vietnam	Saigon, Vietnam
6234	Radio Budapest	Budapest, Hungary
7118	Radio Republik Indonesia	Denpasar, Indonesia
7125	Radio Warsaw	Warsaw, Poland
7125	Radiodiffusion Nationale	Canakry, Guinea
7140	Radio Riga	Riga, USSR
7140	Radio Republik Indonesia	Ambon, Indonesia
7165	Libyan Broadcasting and TV	El Beida, Libya
7170	Radio Noumea	Noumea, New Caledonia
7175	Radio Televisione Italiana	Caltanissetta, Sicily
7200	Radio Omdurman	Omdurman, Sudan
7205	Radio Australia	Melbourne, Australia

Table 7-2. A Schedule of Stations and Frequencies (Cont'd)

Frequency (kHz)	Identification	Location
7220	Radio Australia	Melbourne, Australia
7275	Voice of Nigeria	Lagos, Nigeria
7292	Trans World Radio	Monte Carlo, Monaco
7301	Radio Biafra	Orlu, Biafra
7320	Radio Tirana	Tirana, Albania
7345	Radio Prague	Prague, Czechoslovakia
9009	Kol Israel	Jerusalem, Israel
9475	Radio Cairo	Cairo, Egypt
9505	Radio Japan	Tokyo, Japan
9510	Radio TV Algerienne	Algiers, Algeria
9515	Radio Ankara	Ankara, Turkey
9520	Australian Broadcasting Comm.	Port Moresby, Paupua Terr.
9525	Radio Havana Cuba	Havana, Cuba
9540	Radio New Zealand	Wellington, N. Zealand
9550	Radio Norway	Oslo, Norway
9600	British Broadcasting Corp.	Ascension Island
9610	Voice of Ethiopia	Addis Ababa, Ethiopia
9610	Australian Broadcasting Comm.	Perth, Australia
9613	Radio Pynongyang	Pyongyang, N. Korea
9625	Radio Australia	Darwin, Australia
9645	Vatican Radio	Vatican City
9660	A Voz de Angola	Luanda, Angola
9695	Radio Moscow	Moscow, USSR
9745	Voice of the Andes	Quito, Ecuador
9770	Radio Amazonas	Iquitos, Peru
9915	Radio Peking	Peking, China
11,715	Swiss Broadcasting Corp.	Berne, Switzerland
11,795	World International Broadcasters	Red Lion, Pa., USA
11,815	Radio Free Europe	Lisbon, Portugal
11,835	Evangelistic Voice of West Indies	Cap Haitien, Haiti
11,855	All India Radio	Delhi, India
11,915	Voice of the Andes	Quito, Ecuador
11,940	Radio Bucharest	Bucharest, Rumania
11,949	Radio Vietnam	Saigon, Vietnam
11,950	Radio Nederland	Hilversum, Netherlands
11,975	Windward Is. Broadcasting Service	St. Georges, Grenada
15,125	Voice of Free China	Taipei, Taiwan
15,215	Radio New York Worldwide	New York, N.Y., USA
17,735	Voice of America	Tinang, Philippines

31-, 41-, and 49-Meter Bands

These three bands are grouped together since they perform in a similar manner and include the greatest number of international stations. Here will be found most of the powerful stations from all over the world. The frequencies are open during many hours of the day and evening and provide the richest source of DX for the listener. Signals tend to be strongest during the evening in winter on 49 and 41 meters, while the 31-meter band often holds up well in the evening hours throughout the year.

11-, 13-, 16-, 19-, and 25-Meter Bands

Located in the upper reaches of the radio spectrum, signals on these bands are significantly affected by changes in

Courtesy QST Magazine

Fig. 7-1. Hams operating under field conditions.

sunspot activity and season. The general rule states that when the number of sunspots increases, the higher frequencies are received over longer distances. The 13-, 16-, and 19-meter bands are usually heard during daylight hours; some nighttime listening is possible during the summer. All bands in this region are unstable to the extent that rapid changes in conditions are common.

AMATEUR BANDS

The ham bands are liberally sprinkled throughout the short-wave dial. Many hum with activity as U.S. hams contact each other and their counterparts in other countries. Their ensuing conversations are often technical in nature—signal reports are exchanged, equipment and antennas discussed, and comments given on band conditions. There is, however, plenty of general "rag-chewing" which makes for interesting listening, especially when the "hams" are on a project in the field (Fig. 7-1). Hams often volunteer for emergency communications during disaster. Note the whip antenna on the vehicle at right in Fig. 7-2. This is the identifying mark of a mobile transmitter.

The behavior of the ham frequencies follows that of the conditions described earlier for the SW bands. The 160- and 80-meter bands, for example, are restricted to fairly short-range communications of several hundred miles. Long-haul contacts, extending to many thousands of miles, are usually made on the 40- and 20-meter bands. Higher frequencies also skip considerable distances but are more susceptible to solar activity. The major bands of interest are shown in Table 7-3.

In most instances a portion of each ham band is designated for CW (code) use. This affords an excellent opportunity for code practice by the SWL'er who wishes to acquire a ham license. Careful tuning will provide transmissions at virtually all code speeds. A steady source of

Fig. 7-2. Vehicles at right can be used by hams for emergency messages.

slow-speed signals (approximately five words per minute) is found on the two Novice CW bands of 80 and 40 meters.

CITIZENS BAND

Toward the end of the 1950's the Federal Communications Commission removed the 11-meter band from ham use

Table 7-3. Ham Bands Found on Conventional SW Receiver

Meters	Frequency (kHz)
160	1800 to 2000
80 *	3500 to 4000
40 **	7000 to 7300
20	14,000 to 14,350
15	21,000 to 21,450
10	28,000 to 29,700

* Novice CW—3700 to 3750.
** Novice CW—7175 to 7200.

and reassigned it to a newly created section of the Citizens Radio Service. Popularity known as Class-D Citizens band (CB), it is used for long-range business and personal communications with low-power equipment. The range of CB signals is usually less than 20 miles from the transmitting point, but the great number of stations on the air provide the SWL'er with signals in nearly all parts of the country. CB stations are not permitted to make long-distance contact via skip, but the phenomenon does occur on the 27-MHz frequency allocated to the service. It is not uncommon to hear two CB stations located a thousand or so miles away from the SWL'er talking to each other.

The channels in this service are listed in Table 7-4. These frequencies are labeled on most SW sets, but may be marked "11-meters" or "amateur band" on older models.

Table 7-4. Location of Class-D Citizens Band

Channel	Frequency (kHz)
1	26,965
2	26,975
3	26,985
4	27,005
5	27,015
6	27,025
7	27,035
8	27,055
9	27,065
10	27,075
11	27,085
12	27,105
13	27,115
14	27,125
15	27,135
16	27,155
17	27,165
18	27,175
19	27,185
20	27,205
21	27,215
22	27,225
23	27,255

MARITIME MOBILE BAND

If you wish to tune in on traffic concerned with activity on the water, the spot to find is located near the low end of the dial (2 to 3 MHz). This is where the tugboat captains, private and commercial boats, and the Coast Guard conduct much of their communications. There is ship-to-ship and ship-to-shore activity of many types. Of course the strongest signals are heard when the SW set is located near large bodies of water found on the East, West, and Gulf Coasts and in the Great Lakes area. However, signals do travel considerable distances inland. Much of the interesting activity is from pleasure boat owners. During summer weekends, the marine band is filled with talk such as where the fish are biting. The single most important channel in the band is 2182 kHz. This is the calling and distress frequency monitored by the Coast Guard on a continuous basis.

An important function in the marine band is the broadcasting of weather reports by both commercial and Coast Guard stations. The schedules shown in Table 7-5 give a detailed listing of coastal stations and when they may be heard.

A second marine band that is not included on general-coverage short-wave receivers exists at frequencies in the vhf region. Monitoring vhf marine broadcasts requires a special-coverage receiver, as mentioned in a later section. There are approximately two dozen channels assigned in the 156-157 MHz region for communications between boats and shore stations. The significant frequency in the band is 156.8 MHz, a channel that is continuously monitored by the U. S. Coast Guard for possible distress calls. The range of stations operating in this band is limited to about 20 to 30 miles. Thus, any monitoring must be within a reasonable distance of boating or shipping areas.

You might also hear small-boat owners talking on the 27-MHz CB band because equipment for communicating at

Table 7-5. Locations of Marine Stations Broadcasting Weather Reports

Location	Call Sign	Frequency (kHz)	Local Time
Boston, Mass.	WOU	2450, 2506	0420, 1020, 1120, 1620, 2220
Wilmington, Del.	WEH	2558	0030, 1230
New York, N. Y.	WOX	*2482, 2522, 2590	0015, 1215
Ocean Gate, N. J.	WAQ	2558	0015, 1215
Norfolk, Va.	WGB	*2450, 2538	0500, 1100, 1700, 2300
Charleston, S. C.	WJO	2566	0015, 1215
Jacksonville, Fla.	WNJ	2566	0000, 1200
Miami, Fla.	WDR	2490	0015, 1215
Tampa, Fla.	WFA	2466, *2550	0000, 1200
Mobile, Ala.	WLO	2592	0100, 0300, 0500, 1100, 1300, 1500, 1700, 1900, 2100, 2300
New Orleans, La.	WAK	2482, 2558, 2598	0500, 1400
Galveston, Texas	KQP	2530	0100, 1830
San Francisco, Calif.	KLH	2506, 2450	0430, 1630, 2130
Eureka, Calif.	KOE	2506, 2450	0445, 1645, 2145
Astoria, Oregon	KFX	2598	0515, 1715
Portland, Oregon	KQX	2598	0530, 1730
Coos Bay, Wash.	KTJ	2566	0230, 1730
Seattle, Wash.	KOW	*2482, 2552	0500, 1700

(Following are U.S. Coast Guard Stations. Emergency broadcasts made immediately.)

Location	Call Sign	Frequency (kHz)	Local Time
Boston, Mass.	NMF	2670	0440, 1040, 1640, 2240
New York, N. Y.	NMY	2670	0020, 1220
Cape May, N. J.	NMK	2670	1100, 2300
Baltimore, Md.	NMX	2670	1730
Norfolk, Va.	NMN	2670	0520, 1720
Charleston, S. C.	NMB	2670	0420, 1620
Jacksonville, Fla.	NMV	2670	0620, 1820
Miami, Fla.	NMA	2670	0450, 1650
St. Petersburg, Fla.	NOF	2670	0420, 1620
New Orleans, La.	NMG	2670	0550, 1150, 1750, 2350
Galveston, Texas	NOY	2670	0520, 1120, 1720, 2320
Long Beach, Calif.	NMQ	2670	0500, 1700
San Francisco, Calif.	NMC	2670	0200, 1400
Port Angeles, Calif.	NOW	2670	0545, 1745
West Port, Wash.	NMW	2670	0530, 1730

* Limited operation.

these frequencies is low cost and often portable. A hand held unit is being used by the skipper in Fig. 7-3.

By the time the 1970's draw to a close, the marine band will experience some significant changes. No longer will the pleasure-boat owner be heard on the 2-3 MHz band. These frequencies will be occupied only by commercial and professional boatmen. Further, their signals will be transmitted on *single-sideband* (SSB), a technique that is considerably more efficient than standard a-m (amplitude modulation). The sideband signal not only travels further on a given amount of power, it also enables more stations to occupy a band with less interference.

It also requires a special technique since the sideband signal sounds like gibberish unless it is correctly tuned. The receiver must have a beat frequency oscillator turned on during sideband reception. After the signal is tuned for

Fig. 7-3. Using portable 27-MHz CB equipment for marine communications.

loudest (though unintelligible) sound in the speaker, the bandspread dial must be tuned *very* slowly across the signal. At one very critical point, the signal will convert to clear speech. The same technique is used for tuning ham stations which operate in the sideband mode.

The second marine band, the one in the vhf region just mentioned, will be the province of pleasure craft and other small boats. Signals there will be transmitted via fm, but any SW receiver capable of picking up the band should also accommodate the fm signal. A receiver in this category is shown in Fig. 7-4.

FREQUENCY-STANDARD STATIONS

Dotted throughout the bands are the frequency-standard stations. They provide special services to anyone who wishes

Fig. 7-4. Westinghouse *Model RPM5020* 5-band portable receiver.

to use them. Time signals, reference tones, and propagation reports are transmitted with extreme accuracy. It should be possible to pick up at least one of the channels at any given time, since transmitting power is high.

VHF SPECTRUM

The use of two-way radio has increased tremendously over the past years and daily the spectrum grows more crowded. The situation has assumed such distressing proportions that many of the services the SWL'er wishes to hear are no longer found within the range of basic SW receiver coverage (from 0.5 to 30 MHz). Of particular interest, for example, are the activities of local police and fire departments. In a move to alleviate crowded conditions, the Federal Communications Commission (FCC) has shifted most of these frequencies into the more spacious vhf band (30 MHz to 300 MHz) where the line-of-sight path keeps them fairly short range. This practice allows the same frequency to be assigned to many areas of the country without undue interference.

However, the SWL'er still has access to vhf frequencies if he is willing to purchase the necessary receiving equipment. Individual receivers are generally available to cover each of the most popular vhf bands. A typical unit is shown in Fig. 7-5. Some are dual-band models, which cover two of the major bands.

Another method for receiving vhf is to add a converter to a conventional a-m radio or short-wave receiver. As its name implies, a converter is an accessory that changes the vhf signal to a frequency which can be picked up on a conventional a-m or short-wave receiver. Converters are usually restricted to a small portion of any given band (often a 1-MHz segment). For this reason, it is advisable to learn in advance which frequency or channels you wish to monitor before ordering the converter. In many instances you must inform the converter manufacturer of the desired frequency since a suitable receiving crystal must be factory installed. The three major vhf bands are divided into these frequency groupings:

30-50 MHz Medium range police communications, radio paging systems, mobile telephone, industrial communications, and other services.

108-135 MHz Aircraft in flight and aircraft control towers. (Note: Other aircraft frequencies are covered on hf [3-30 MHz], especially for long-range flights.)

150-174 MHz Police, fire departments, marine emergency services, mobile telephone, taxicabs, trucks, and others.

Fig. 7-5. Hallicrafters *Portamon* receiver covering 140 to 174 MHz.

Notice that there is some overlap in assigning certain services in more than one band. Table 7-6 shows a chart of the various categories and frequencies on vhf.

If you are unable to find out the frequency of the local police or fire department, there is a way of approximating it, at least to the degree of discovering the band to which it is assigned. The method relies on the fact that the whip antenna is cut to the operating frequency. (As discussed in the chapter on antennas, a given frequency is received best with a discrete antenna length.) First step is to judge the

Table 7-6. Services on VHF (30 to 300 MHz)

Frequency Allocation (MHz)	Services
30 — 50 MHz BAND	
30.56 - 32	Industrial, land transportation, public safety
33 - 34	Public safety, industrial, land transportation
35 - 36	Industrial, domestic public
37 - 38	Public safety, industrial
39 - 40	Public safety
40 - 42	Industrial, scientific and medical equipment
42 - 50	Public safety, industrial, domestic public, land transportation.
108 — 135 MHz BAND	
108 - 118	Aeronautical radionavigation
118 - 132	Aeronautical mobile: control towers, private aircraft, commercial aircraft, flight tests and schools, utility.
150 — 174 MHz BAND	
150 - 174	Land transportation, public safety, industrial, domestic, public, maritime mobile.

Classification

Aeronautical—Commercial and private aircraft, ground stations.

Industrial—Power, petroleum, forest products, news services, motion picture studios, businesses, construction, farming.

Land Transportation—Common and contract carriers of freight and passengers; railroad, taxi, motor carrier, auto emergency.

Public Safety—Police, fire, forestry, highway maintenance, disaster relief, physicians in rural areas, ambulance, rescue.

Maritime—Commercial and private stations in marine activities.

length, in feet, of the whip as closely as possible. Then divide this length into 234. The answer reveals the approximate frequency in megahertz. For example, if the whip appears to be about six feet in height, the frequency is roughly 39 MHz (234 divided by 6). This places it within the 30- to 50-MHz band. On higher bands whips are far shorter, but still adhere to the same formula. (The method is based on the fact that mobile whips are customarily designed to be one-quarter the physical length of the radio wave.)

VERY-LOW–FREQUENCY SPECTRUM

The very-low–frequency (vlf) band, along with vhf, is not included on the conventional short-wave set. Occupying the space below the standard a-m broadcasting band, the channels are principally assigned to radio-range beacon stations. The only reason for mentioning the band is that vlf coverage is sometimes found on the two- and three-band transistor portable marketed for the small boat owner. These sets usually have movable loop antennas which enable the operator to "home in" on the vlf signal for radio direction finding.

Another useful aspect of the band is that it provides a steady source of weather information. The listing given in Table 7-7 comprises stations that operate on a 24-hour daily schedule and transmit weather reports every 15 and 45 minutes after the hour.

LOGS AND RECORDINGS

The pleasure of short-wave listening is enhanced by keeping a log. It is a handy record, usually in the form of a notebook, in which information is noted for future reference. Stations heard, comments about programming, times, frequencies—all may be charted as suggested in Fig. 7-6. Not only is it interesting to reread months later, but it serves a

Table 7-7. VLF Stations Broadcasting Weather Information*

Location	Call Letters	Frequency (kHz)
East Coast		
Bangor, Maine	BGR	239
Hartford, Conn.	HFD	329
Boston, Mass.	SEW	382
Newark, N. J.	EWR	379
Millville, N. J.	MIV	365
Washington, D. C.	DC	332
Charleston, S. C.	CH	329
Jacksonville, Fla.	JAX	344
Miami, Fla.	MF	365
San Juan, Puerto Rico	SJU	391
Gulf Coast		
Key West, Fla.	EYW	332
St. Petersburg, Fla.	AMP	388
Pensacola, Fla.	PNS	326
Mobile, Alabama	MO	248
New Orleans, La.	GNI	236
Galveston, Texas	GLS	206
Pacific Coast		
Los Angeles, Calif.	LAX	332
Oakland, Calif.	OAK	362
Portland, Ore.	PDX	332
Seattle, Wash.	SEA	362

* Weather reports are broadcast 15 and 45 minutes after the hour, 24 hours a day.

(YEAR)						
STATION	LOCATION	TIME	FREQUENCY	DATE	RECEPTION QUALITY	REMARKS

Fig. 7-6. Headings for radio log.

79

practical purpose as well. A detailed log will contain current information on operating schedules and frequencies announced over the air. It is fine for recounting to friends and family the fascinating DX picked up during the wee hours of the morning.

A tape recorder is another handy accessory that can re-create for others the exciting events heard on the bands. If one is readily available, it is a simple matter to record broadcasts off the air. Use the setup shown in Fig. 7-7. A pair of

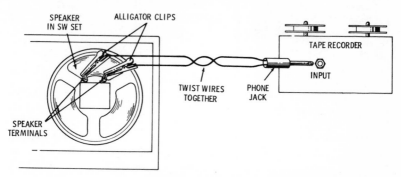

Fig. 7-7. Recording short-wave programs on tape.

wires is clipped to the speaker lugs of the short-wave receiver and terminated at the input of the tape recorder. (Use the "phono" or "tuner" input on the machine.) With this system, the normal sound from the set is undisturbed. If you hear hum in the recording, reverse the two clip leads to the speaker lugs.

QSL CARDS

Collecting colorful verification reports from SW stations is a highly prized activity among short-wave listeners. Known as QSL cards, they are sent out by stations to listeners who wish to verify the fact that the signal was received. They make an interesting display gleaned from all

Fig. 7-8. Colorful QSL cards from SW stations.

parts of the world when tacked on the wall, as shown in Fig. 7-8.

To obtain QSL's, the short-wave listener should prepare a brief but detailed report of conditions which existed at the time the signal was received. Accuracy is important; the information is of technical value to the stations in checking their coverage area. As shown in Fig. 7-9, stations are interested in gathering reports and data on radio propagation.

Courtesy Radio Free Europe

Fig. 7-9. Engineer at SW station charts frequencies and band conditions to help improve reception.

Your report, in card or letter form, should contain the following information:

1. The exact time (local or GMT) of reception.
2. Date of reception.
3. Frequency.
4. Program identification.
   This may be the name of the program or a word description. Include subject matter, titles of musical selections, or other identifying features.
5. Radio conditions.
   Describe reception in terms of strength: strong, good, fair, poor, or unusable. Was interference absent, slight, moderate, severe, or extreme? What was the nature of the interference—code, other station, static, or fading?
6. Receiving equipment.
   Name your receiver and antenna type.
7. Request QSL card or verification report.

In the case of international broadcast stations, return postage is not always required. However, the greatest response occurs if you include an International Reply Coupon with all requests, especially for nonbroadcast services. Such coupons are available at your local post office and may be exchanged by the station to whom you send them for postage. Remember, do not send stamps for return postage, since U.S. stamps will not be valid in the country to which you send the letter.

OTHER AIDS

An excellent publication for the SWL'er is available from the U.S. Government Printing Office. It is a booklet which gives a listing of radio-frequency allocations agreed on by internationual treaty. Covering the spectrum from 10 kHz to over 170 MHz, it shows which segments are assigned to various broadcasts and communications services. A copy may be secured by writing to: Superintendent of Documents, U. S. Government Printing Office, Washington, D.C. 20402. Ask for Vol. 2 of FCC Rules and Regulations. It will also contain information about other radio services which are not necessarily of interest to the SWL'er. It is not possible, however, to order only the section which pertains to frequencies (Part 2).

From the same address you can secure "Broadcasting Stations of the World," a publication of the U.S. Information Agency.

The U.S. Government also makes available predictions of radio conditions by the National Bureau of Standards. The reports are mailed monthly for a yearly charge. Request "Central Radio Propagation Laboratory Bulletin; National Bureau of Standards." The address again is that of the U.S. Government Printing Office.

Other publications and current reports of SW activities are found in the pages of the various electronics magazines sold on the newsstands.

CHAPTER 8

Signals From Space

A new era in short-wave listening was introduced with the launchings of space vehicles. Equipped with miniature transmitting equipment, orbiting satellites were soon discovered to emit radio signals that could be picked up on home-type equipment. The field has grown to provide new challenges for the DX hunter who wishes to expand his horizons to outer space. Unlike casual tuning on the conventional bands, monitoring spacecraft calls for new skills and knowledge on the part of the hobbyist.

Most of the current listening is concerned with identifying the source of assorted beeps, clicks, and rushing sounds that make up space-vehicle transmissions. The signal is usually a complex one, comprised of data channels which send the various measurements acquired by the craft back to earth. It is usually beyond the capability of the SWL'er to interpret the composition of the signal; however, the actual monitoring of the signal provides the reward.

Another aspect of space communications is the supporting network of ground stations. They often transmit on frequencies within the coverage of a conventional SW receiver. It is especially interesting to listen to these ground stations during manned space flights. Signals via skip from ground stations permit monitoring of such activities as launch preparations and recovery. The frequencies assigned for this purpose are 20.00-20.01 MHz.

The principal requirement for tuning satellites is equipment that will receive the proper frequencies since most of them operate in the vhf and uhf bands. Frequency assignments for meterological satellites are 137.0-138.0 MHz, 1660-1670 MHz, 1690-1700 MHz, and 7.300-7.750 GHz; for radio-navigation satellites, 149.9-150.05 MHz, 399.9-400.05 MHz, and 14.30-14.40 GHz. Receiving any of these requires equipment that is capable of picking up signals considerably above the normal short-wave bands. One approach that is popular is the use of a converter. This is a device that is attached to the antenna terminals of the conventional short-wave set and converts the received signal from vhf to hf. Whatever the system, a crystal calibrator is indispensable. The low power of spacecraft transmitters, often a few thousandths of a watt, means tuning must be "on the nose."

In the area of antennas, good results have been achieved with the simple, single wire setups discussed earlier. Emphasis should be on length; the longer the antenna the broader its pickup pattern tends to be. After some experience is acquired, the SWL'er may wish to experiment with high-gain directional antennas precisely cut for the exact frequency of reception. However, it should be noted that most spacecraft are constantly in motion and create tracking problems when highly directional antennas are used.

Some of the communications satellites (for example, Early Bird), are in synchronous orbit, which means they apparently hover at a fixed point. Although these satellites would provide choice listening, this is not yet practical for the home hobbyist. To achieve synchronous orbit the satellite must be more than 22,000 miles high. This calls for an extremely sophisticated antenna system. In addition, the signals are transmitted in the microwave region (millions of megahertz), and suitable receiving equipment is now impractical for the SW hobbyist.

Telemetry signals from orbiting satellites are literally snared on the run. As a vehicle circles the earth, reception time is a few minutes' duration in any given region. Best results occur if the receiver is warmed up and on frequency just prior to an expected "pass" over your region. This information can be secured from published reports in newspapers and scientific magazines. Look to these sources, too, for timely information on frequencies. On the regular shortwave bands it is often announced by Radio Moscow for Soviet space activities. Information on U. S. space flights is sometimes available from the Office of Public Information, NASA, Washington, D.C. 20546.

Once you are certain that the receiver is properly calibrated and the satellite is due to appear shortly, the bfo is turned on. (This is the same control used for code reception.) This signal mixes with the incoming satellite carrier within the receiver to produce an audible tone. The most characteristic feature of the sound is that it changes in pitch due to the Doppler effect. As illustrated in Fig. 8-1, an approaching spacecraft is emitting a radio carrier on a fixed frequency. However, the forward movement of the craft *adds* to the speed of the transmitted radio wave. The effect is that of compressing cycles together and raising the total number which occur each second. Thus, the receiver on the ground picks up energy which is slightly higher in frequency than the actual wave broadcast from the satellite antenna. As the vehicle passes overhead and achieves the "point of closest approach," the true frequency is received. Under this condition, forward speed is not added as before. The opposite result occurs when the signal moves away from the listening point. Movement of the receding satellite now subtracts from the speed of the wave as it travels back toward the receiver.

What the listener hears during these phases when the satellite is "acquired" is a rising tone on the approach that is followed by a lowering of the tone after it passes by. The basic effect is identical to the familiar example of a passing

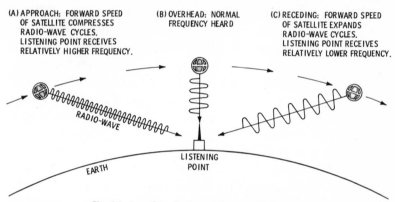

(A) APPROACH: FORWARD SPEED OF SATELLITE COMPRESSES RADIO-WAVE CYCLES. LISTENING POINT RECEIVES RELATIVELY HIGHER FREQUENCY.

(B) OVERHEAD: NORMAL FREQUENCY HEARD

(C) RECEDING: FORWARD SPEED OF SATELLITE EXPANDS RADIO-WAVE CYCLES. LISTENING POINT RECEIVES RELATIVELY LOWER FREQUENCY.

RADIO-WAVE

EARTH

LISTENING POINT

Fig. 8-1. Doppler effect on radio wave from space.

railroad train. The rise and fall in the pitch of the whistle may also be explained by the Doppler effect on sound waves.

The apparent shift in satellite frequency is not very great, often on the order of several thousand cycles. With the receiver tuned to the exact center frequency of the satellite transmitter, the resulting tone in the speaker changes over a band within the range of human hearing. Again, it should be noted that other sounds may be superimposed on the satellite signal. Many forms of intelligence are impressed on the basic carrier to represent telemetered data.

CHAPTER 9

Hints on Maintaining Your SW Set

With the passage of time the SW receiver may experience a gradual or sudden deterioration in performance. Many of the problems can be solved only by a competent serviceman and expensive test equipment. However, there are simpler problems which the SWL'er may correct.

Any steps which require removal of the chassis from its cabinet should be approached with caution. Voltages in the circuits may run as high as 250 volts and could cause dangerous shock. The line cord must always be removed completely from the ac outlet before any work is done in this area. Unless you have the skill and equipment, none of the tuning screws inside the cabinet should be touched. Rarely will these adjustments get out of alignment.

NOISE

Many troubles give the appearance of originating inside the receiver, but are actually generated externally. The principal problem of this type is man-made electrical noise. It arises from the operation of motors, household appliances, TV sets, automobiles, and other devices that cause either sparking or a sudden change in the amount of electrical current. In the majority of cases noise appears directly on radio frequencies and rides into the receiver through the antenna or power line.

A simple test is to disconnect the antenna from the set. If noise drops, it is an indication that it is entering via the antenna. This should not be confused with the normal atmospheric level which produces a steady hiss at all times. What you are listening for is a quieting of clicks, buzzes, and other sounds which occur during those intervals when the noise-generating device is at work. The sparking of an oil burner, vacuum cleaner, electric shaver, or pump, for example, are intermittent in nature.

There are two approaches to curing noise induced into the antenna. The first is height; the higher the wire, the less susceptible it becomes to noise pickup. Man-made interference tends to occur at or near the ground. In bad cases, converting to a coaxial cable transmission line (see Chapter 5) is another technique. The shielded braid of the cable is immune to noise energy between the receiver and antenna proper. Another measure is to avoid the use of vertical antennas because they are more sensitive to noise pickup than the horizontal wire.

Yet another plan of attack is to reduce noise pickup by filtering at the offending source. This is impractical for passing automobiles, but it is useful for appliances in the home. If interference is serious, you might have a serviceman install a filter inside the noisy appliance. This can be done, for example, in an oil burner for a home heating system. The electrical ignition in the burner can, in some cases, produce receiver noise. Another prolific noise generator is the fluorescent lamp as it ionizes gas in the tube at the rate of 60 times per second. There are also "hash" filters available for reducing this type of radiation.

Noise may also gain entry into the receiver through an ac cord. Try reversing the line cord in the wall socket. If this doesn't improve reception, some means of bypassing the noise should be tried. A line-cord filter that plugs into the wall socket is available for the purpose. In stubborn cases of noise, you might have to install the costly kind of filter which contains coils. Such filters usually require a good electrical ground to operate effectively.

Many noise sources transmit energy in both major patterns, through the air to the antenna and via the power line. Thus, a combination of suppression techniques must often be employed, as in the case of interference from a television. TV sets contain a horizontal oscillator that is a vigorous producer of harmonic energy over much of the SW spectrum. This interference is heard as a harsh buzz that pops in and out as the SW tuning dial is rotated. If the measures already described do not cut the interference, one possibility is to relocate the SW set in another room. With TV sets and fluorescent lamps additional distance from the SW receiver often reduces noise considerably.

If the receiver has a noise limiter, it can do much to minimize all types of sharp, pulse-type interference, especially from auto ignition systems. In spite of this, the preceding noise-reducing measures are worth the effort. Since the noise limiter may introduce some amount of distortion into the sound at the speaker, it should be reserved primarily for use when noise is extremely severe.

INTERNAL PROBLEMS

Now look at some common defects which occur in the circuitry of a receiver and what to do before seeking professional help.

Tubes

As in any piece of electronic equipment, tubes are responsible for well over half of the troubles. Since defective tubes can cause virtually every known symptom—like hum, distortion, or a totally dead set—they should be checked first. The principal cause of a tube defect is an open filament. If your set is designed for ac operation only, the defect is often apparent; the tube won't light and feels cool to the touch. In ac-dc sets, the failure of *any* tube removes power to all tubes and pilot lamp, necessitating a complete check. Less obvious faults show up only by substituting with a known good tube or testing on a high-quality tube checker (of the mutual-conductance type). Tests of this type uncover such problems as partial shorts between elements which cause hum and small changes in tubes that produce a loss of sensitivity.

One elusive problem concerns the local-oscillator tube; it may test good but cause the receiver to malfunction. The symptom to note is good receiver performance on low bands with failure on the higher frequencies. Another sign is that some atmospheric noise is heard on the higher bands, though no signals are received.

Aging tubes may perform well but produce a ringing sound in the speaker. This is a microphonic condition that occurs when loose tube elements are set into mechanical movement by the speaker vibrating or other physical disturbance reaching the chassis.

A profusion of ruggedly constructed tube types of superior performance is available to use in place of existing ones in the set. In replacing tubes, follow the recommendation of a reliable guide such as the *Tube Substitution Handbook* published by Howard W. Sams & Co., Inc.

Semiconductors

Many receivers now being manufactured use transistors and diodes in place of tubes. The failure rate of these parts is very low, so no periodic testing is necessary. They should only be replaced by qualified servicemen.

When receivers are battery powered, a new battery should be tried first when unsatisfactory operation is experienced.

92

If the receiver is equipped to operate on an alternate source of power, a quick check can be made by switching to it. Satisfactory operation is a sure sign that the battery supply is defective and should be replaced.

Tuning Capacitors

Dirt, grease, and corrosion take their toll on the tuning capacitor. This is the component with two or three moving-plate sections driven by the main tuning knob. A similar but smaller capacitor is used for the bandspread. Signs of trouble in this area include: a scratching sound when you are tuning on any band, no signals at some points in the tuning range, or a completely dead receiver. Careful cleaning of these variable capacitors often cures the problem. This may be done by blowing air between the plates, then brushing with a radio-type solvent. One important area is at the wiper contacts of the capacitor bearing. Finally, check for tightness of the capacitor mounting screws. Sometimes these screws pass through rubber shock absorbers that can cause microphonics if they have hardened with age.

Controls and Contacts

As one of the frequently used parts in the set, the volume control is subject to damaging wear. The earliest sign is a scratching sound as the knob is rotated. When the condition worsens, noise might occur with no movement of the control. A technique which greatly extends the life of the part is the injection of liquid contact cleaner. Introduce it into the small spaces between the lugs on the control while rotating the knob rapidly back and forth.

The same treatment may be given other mechanical components which accumulate dust and dirt. Also apply contact cleaner to all switches and controls.

Another troublesome area is the space between lugs on all tube sockets. Foreign matter accumulates here and sets up an electrical path which affects receiver performance. With a soft brush dipped in the liquid contact cleaner go over every visible socket space and flush it clean.

AC Cord

The greatest point of stress on the power cord is where it meets the ac plug. Any sign of cracking or fraying of the insulation here should be corrected before a short circuit or shock hazard develops. Replace the cord completely with conventional lamp cord except in the case of some old ac-dc sets. (These models sometimes have a resistance wire built into the cord and must be renewed with an identical replacement part.)

Dial Cord

Slippage of a pointer can often be traced to the dial cord. If the problem is slight, a special dial-cord dressing usually corrects the condition. More pronounced cases yield to a small amount of tightening of the spring that holds one end of the cord to a tuning drum. If the cord is broken or stretched beyond adjustment, it should be replaced—but never without the stringing diagram. Otherwise, hours will be spent in trying to figure out the loops and circles the cord is supposed to follow.

OTHER PROBLEMS

Speakers develop defects which cause distortion in sound reproduction. Gently touch the center of the paper cone with a fingertip and push it in a fraction of an inch. If you feel any rubbing, the speaker is ready for replacement. Small tears in the paper cone may be repaired with clear cement. Cabinets, dial windows, speaker grilles, and other parts loosen with age and should be retightened periodically. Unless they are mounted securely, they are likely to produce hard-to-trace noise of a mechanical or electrical nature.

Index